50 Delicious Chocolate Cooking Dishes

By: Kelly Johnson

Table of Contents

- Chocolate Lava Cake
- Chocolate Mousse
- Chocolate Chip Cookies
- Chocolate Brownies
- Chocolate Truffles
- Chocolate Fondue
- Chocolate Cake
- Chocolate Fudge
- Chocolate Cupcakes
- Chocolate Pudding
- Chocolate Cheesecake
- Chocolate Tart
- Hot Chocolate
- Chocolate Dipped Strawberries
- Chocolate Croissants
- Chocolate Ice Cream
- Chocolate Milkshake
- Chocolate Eclairs
- Chocolate Soufflé

- Chocolate Caramel Bars
- Chocolate Ganache
- Chocolate Chip Pancakes
- Chocolate Covered Pretzels
- Chocolate Coconut Balls
- Chocolate Popcorn
- Chocolate Panna Cotta
- Chocolate Mocha Cake
- Chocolate Hazelnut Spread
- Chocolate Chip Scones
- Chocolate Dipped Marshmallows
- Chocolate Biscotti
- Chocolate Covered Almonds
- Chocolate Coconut Macaroons
- Chocolate Ice Cream Sandwiches
- Chocolate Peanut Butter Cups
- Chocolate Babka
- Chocolate Meringues
- Chocolate Fudge Cake
- White and Dark Chocolate Swirl Cheesecake
- Chocolate and Raspberry Tart

- Chocolate Coconut Pudding
- Chocolate Almond Bark
- Chocolate Coconut Truffles
- Chocolate Chip Banana Bread
- Chocolate Cheesecake Bars
- Chocolate Chia Pudding
- Chocolate Tiramisu
- Chocolate Pretzel Bark
- Chocolate Almond Croissants
- Chocolate Soufflé Cake

Chocolate Lava Cake

Ingredients:

- 1/2 cup unsalted butter
- 6 oz bittersweet chocolate, chopped
- 1 cup powdered sugar
- 2 large eggs
- 2 egg yolks
- 1 tsp vanilla extract
- 1/4 cup all-purpose flour
- Pinch of salt
- Butter and cocoa powder for greasing ramekins

Instructions:

1. Preheat the oven to 425°F (220°C). Butter and dust four ramekins with cocoa powder.
2. In a heatproof bowl, melt butter and chocolate together over a double boiler or in the microwave. Stir until smooth.
3. Whisk in powdered sugar, then eggs, egg yolks, and vanilla extract.
4. Fold in flour and salt.
5. Pour the batter evenly into the prepared ramekins.
6. Bake for 12-14 minutes, until the edges are set but the center is still soft.
7. Let cool for 1 minute, then carefully run a knife around the edges and invert onto plates. Serve immediately.

Chocolate Mousse

Ingredients:

- 8 oz bittersweet chocolate, chopped
- 2 tbsp butter
- 1 1/2 cups heavy cream
- 1/4 cup powdered sugar
- 1 tsp vanilla extract

Instructions:

1. Melt chocolate and butter in a heatproof bowl over simmering water (double boiler).
2. In a separate bowl, whip heavy cream with powdered sugar until stiff peaks form.
3. Gently fold the melted chocolate into the whipped cream, adding vanilla extract.
4. Spoon mousse into serving dishes and refrigerate for at least 2 hours before serving.

Chocolate Chip Cookies

Ingredients:

- 2 1/4 cups all-purpose flour
- 1 tsp baking soda
- 1/2 tsp salt
- 1 cup unsalted butter, softened
- 1 cup brown sugar
- 1/2 cup granulated sugar
- 2 large eggs
- 2 tsp vanilla extract
- 2 cups semisweet chocolate chips

Instructions:

1. Preheat the oven to 350°F (175°C).
2. In a bowl, mix flour, baking soda, and salt.
3. In a large bowl, cream together butter, brown sugar, and granulated sugar.
4. Beat in eggs, one at a time, and then add vanilla extract.
5. Gradually mix in dry ingredients until combined.
6. Stir in chocolate chips.
7. Drop rounded tablespoons of dough onto a baking sheet and bake for 9-11 minutes, until golden. Cool on wire racks.

Chocolate Brownies

Ingredients:

- 1 cup unsalted butter
- 8 oz bittersweet chocolate, chopped
- 1 1/4 cups granulated sugar
- 3/4 cup brown sugar
- 4 large eggs
- 1 tsp vanilla extract
- 1 cup all-purpose flour
- 1/4 tsp salt

Instructions:

1. Preheat the oven to 350°F (175°C). Grease a 9x13-inch baking pan.
2. Melt butter and chocolate together in a heatproof bowl over a double boiler.
3. Stir in sugars, then add eggs and vanilla.
4. Fold in flour and salt until combined.
5. Pour the batter into the pan and bake for 30-35 minutes, until a toothpick comes out with a few moist crumbs. Cool before cutting.

Chocolate Truffles

Ingredients:

- 8 oz bittersweet chocolate, chopped
- 1/2 cup heavy cream
- 1/4 cup unsalted butter
- Cocoa powder, crushed nuts, or melted chocolate for coating

Instructions:

1. Heat the cream and butter in a saucepan until simmering.
2. Pour over chopped chocolate and let sit for 5 minutes. Stir until smooth.
3. Refrigerate the mixture for 1-2 hours until firm.
4. Scoop out small portions and roll them into balls.
5. Coat with cocoa powder, crushed nuts, or dip in melted chocolate. Refrigerate until set.

Chocolate Fondue

Ingredients:

- 8 oz milk chocolate, chopped
- 1/2 cup heavy cream
- 1 tbsp butter
- 1 tsp vanilla extract

Instructions:

1. Heat cream and butter in a saucepan until simmering.
2. Pour over chopped chocolate and let sit for 2-3 minutes. Stir until smooth.
3. Add vanilla extract and stir to combine.
4. Serve with fruit, marshmallows, or cake for dipping.

Chocolate Cake

Ingredients:

- 1 3/4 cups all-purpose flour
- 1 1/2 cups granulated sugar
- 3/4 cup unsweetened cocoa powder
- 1 1/2 tsp baking powder
- 1 1/2 tsp baking soda
- 1 tsp salt
- 2 large eggs
- 1 cup milk
- 1/2 cup vegetable oil
- 1 tsp vanilla extract
- 1 cup boiling water

Instructions:

1. Preheat the oven to 350°F (175°C). Grease and flour two 9-inch round cake pans.
2. Mix together all dry ingredients.
3. Add eggs, milk, oil, and vanilla extract. Beat for 2 minutes.
4. Stir in the boiling water (batter will be thin).
5. Pour the batter into the pans and bake for 30-35 minutes.
6. Cool and frost as desired.

Chocolate Fudge

Ingredients:

- 2 cups semisweet chocolate chips
- 1 can (14 oz) sweetened condensed milk
- 1 tsp vanilla extract

Instructions:

1. In a saucepan, melt chocolate chips with sweetened condensed milk over low heat, stirring until smooth.
2. Stir in vanilla extract.
3. Pour the mixture into a greased 9x9-inch pan and refrigerate for at least 2 hours.
4. Cut into squares and serve.

Chocolate Cupcakes

Ingredients:

- 1 3/4 cups all-purpose flour
- 3/4 cup unsweetened cocoa powder
- 1 1/2 tsp baking powder
- 1/2 tsp baking soda
- 1/2 tsp salt
- 2 large eggs
- 1 cup granulated sugar
- 1/2 cup vegetable oil
- 1 tsp vanilla extract
- 1 cup milk

Instructions:

1. Preheat the oven to 350°F (175°C). Line a muffin tin with paper liners.
2. In a bowl, whisk together the dry ingredients.
3. In a separate bowl, whisk eggs, sugar, oil, and vanilla.
4. Gradually add the dry ingredients, alternating with milk.
5. Fill cupcake liners 2/3 full and bake for 18-20 minutes.
6. Cool and frost as desired.

Chocolate Pudding

Ingredients:

- 2 cups whole milk
- 1/2 cup granulated sugar
- 1/4 cup unsweetened cocoa powder
- 3 tbsp cornstarch
- 1/8 tsp salt
- 2 large egg yolks
- 2 tbsp unsalted butter
- 1 tsp vanilla extract

Instructions:

1. In a saucepan, whisk together milk, sugar, cocoa powder, cornstarch, and salt.
2. Bring to a simmer over medium heat while stirring constantly.
3. In a separate bowl, whisk egg yolks. Gradually add a small amount of the hot mixture to temper the eggs, then pour it back into the saucepan.
4. Continue to cook for 2-3 minutes until thickened.
5. Remove from heat and stir in butter and vanilla.
6. Pour into serving dishes and refrigerate for at least 2 hours before serving.

Chocolate Cheesecake

Ingredients:

- 1 1/2 cups graham cracker crumbs
- 1/4 cup sugar
- 1/2 cup unsalted butter, melted
- 3 cups cream cheese, softened
- 1 cup granulated sugar
- 1/2 cup sour cream
- 4 large eggs
- 8 oz bittersweet chocolate, melted
- 1 tsp vanilla extract
- Pinch of salt

Instructions:

1. Preheat oven to 325°F (163°C).
2. Combine graham cracker crumbs, sugar, and melted butter. Press into the bottom of a springform pan.
3. Beat cream cheese and sugar until smooth. Add eggs one at a time, followed by sour cream, melted chocolate, vanilla, and salt.
4. Pour filling into crust and bake for 55-60 minutes, or until the center is set.
5. Cool at room temperature, then refrigerate for at least 4 hours before serving.

Chocolate Tart

Ingredients:

- 1 1/2 cups all-purpose flour
- 1/4 cup cocoa powder
- 1/2 cup unsalted butter, chilled and cubed
- 1/4 cup powdered sugar
- 1 large egg
- 1/4 tsp salt
- 8 oz semisweet chocolate
- 1/2 cup heavy cream
- 1/2 tsp vanilla extract

Instructions:

1. Preheat oven to 350°F (175°C).
2. In a food processor, combine flour, cocoa powder, butter, sugar, egg, and salt. Pulse until dough forms.
3. Roll out dough and press into a tart pan. Bake for 15-20 minutes.
4. For the filling, heat cream until simmering, then pour over chopped chocolate. Stir until smooth.
5. Pour filling into baked crust and chill for 2 hours.

Hot Chocolate

Ingredients:

- 2 cups whole milk
- 2 tbsp unsweetened cocoa powder
- 2 tbsp granulated sugar
- 1/2 tsp vanilla extract
- Whipped cream or marshmallows (optional)

Instructions:

1. In a small saucepan, whisk together cocoa powder and sugar. Add milk and cook over medium heat, stirring constantly, until hot.
2. Stir in vanilla extract and pour into a mug.
3. Top with whipped cream or marshmallows if desired.

Chocolate Dipped Strawberries

Ingredients:

- 1 lb fresh strawberries
- 8 oz semisweet chocolate
- 2 tbsp vegetable oil (optional)

Instructions:

1. Wash strawberries and pat dry, leaving the stems on.
2. Melt chocolate with vegetable oil in a heatproof bowl over simmering water or in the microwave in 30-second intervals.
3. Dip each strawberry into the melted chocolate, letting excess drip off.
4. Place on a parchment-lined baking sheet and refrigerate for 30 minutes until set.

Chocolate Croissants

Ingredients:

- 1 package puff pastry sheets
- 1/2 cup semisweet chocolate chips
- 1 egg (for egg wash)
- Powdered sugar (optional)

Instructions:

1. Preheat oven to 375°F (190°C).
2. Roll out puff pastry and cut into triangles.
3. Place a few chocolate chips at the base of each triangle and roll up into croissant shapes.
4. Brush with egg wash and bake for 15-20 minutes until golden.
5. Dust with powdered sugar before serving.

Chocolate Ice Cream

Ingredients:

- 2 cups heavy cream
- 1 cup whole milk
- 3/4 cup granulated sugar
- 1/2 cup unsweetened cocoa powder
- 4 large egg yolks
- 1 tsp vanilla extract
- 8 oz bittersweet chocolate, chopped

Instructions:

1. Heat milk, cream, and sugar in a saucepan.
2. Whisk egg yolks in a bowl. Slowly pour hot cream mixture into egg yolks, whisking constantly.
3. Return the mixture to the pan and cook over low heat until thickened.
4. Stir in cocoa powder and chopped chocolate until melted.
5. Cool the mixture, then churn in an ice cream maker according to manufacturer's instructions.

Chocolate Milkshake

Ingredients:

- 3 cups vanilla ice cream
- 1 cup milk
- 2 tbsp chocolate syrup
- Whipped cream (optional)

Instructions:

1. Blend ice cream, milk, and chocolate syrup until smooth.
2. Pour into a glass and top with whipped cream if desired.

Chocolate Eclairs

Ingredients:

- 1/2 cup unsalted butter
- 1 cup water
- 1 cup all-purpose flour
- 4 large eggs
- 1 1/2 cups heavy cream
- 1/2 cup powdered sugar
- 8 oz semisweet chocolate

Instructions:

1. Preheat oven to 425°F (220°C).
2. In a saucepan, bring butter and water to a boil. Stir in flour until dough forms.
3. Remove from heat and beat in eggs one at a time.
4. Spoon dough onto a baking sheet in 4-inch strips. Bake for 25 minutes.
5. For the filling, whip heavy cream with powdered sugar and pipe into cooled eclairs.
6. Melt chocolate and drizzle over eclairs before serving.

Chocolate Soufflé

Ingredients:

- 6 oz semisweet chocolate
- 2 tbsp unsalted butter
- 1/4 cup granulated sugar, plus more for dusting
- 3 large eggs, separated
- 1/2 tsp vanilla extract
- 1/4 tsp salt

Instructions:

1. Preheat oven to 375°F (190°C). Butter and sugar four ramekins.
2. Melt chocolate and butter in a heatproof bowl.
3. Beat egg yolks with sugar until thickened. Stir in melted chocolate and vanilla.
4. Whisk egg whites with salt until stiff peaks form, then fold into the chocolate mixture.
5. Spoon the batter into ramekins and bake for 12-15 minutes, until puffed and set.
6. Serve immediately.

Chocolate Caramel Bars

Ingredients:

- 1 1/2 cups all-purpose flour
- 1 cup unsalted butter, softened
- 1/2 cup granulated sugar
- 1/2 tsp baking powder
- 1/4 tsp salt
- 1/2 cup caramel sauce
- 8 oz semisweet chocolate, chopped

Instructions:

1. Preheat oven to 350°F (175°C).
2. Beat together butter, sugar, flour, baking powder, and salt until combined.
3. Press the dough into a greased 9x9-inch baking dish.
4. Bake for 20-25 minutes until golden.
5. While baking, melt the caramel sauce and chocolate.
6. Pour the melted caramel over the baked crust, then spread the melted chocolate on top.
7. Chill for 1 hour before cutting into bars.

White and Dark Chocolate Swirl Cheesecake

Ingredients:

- 1 1/2 cups graham cracker crumbs
- 1/4 cup sugar
- 1/2 cup melted butter
- 3 packages (8 oz) cream cheese, softened
- 3/4 cup sugar
- 1 tsp vanilla extract
- 3 eggs
- 1/2 cup sour cream
- 4 oz dark chocolate, melted
- 4 oz white chocolate, melted

Instructions:

1. Preheat oven to 325°F (160°C). Grease a 9-inch springform pan.
2. Mix graham cracker crumbs, sugar, and melted butter together. Press into the bottom of the pan.
3. In a bowl, beat cream cheese and sugar until smooth. Add vanilla and eggs one at a time, mixing well.
4. Fold in sour cream.
5. Pour half of the cheesecake mixture into the pan. Drizzle with melted dark chocolate and swirl with a knife.
6. Pour the remaining cheesecake mixture on top, followed by the melted white chocolate. Swirl again.

Chocolate Fudge Cake

Ingredients:

- 1 1/2 cups all-purpose flour
- 1 1/2 tsp baking powder
- 1/2 tsp baking soda
- 1/2 tsp salt
- 3/4 cup unsweetened cocoa powder
- 1 cup sugar
- 2 large eggs
- 1/2 cup vegetable oil
- 1 tsp vanilla extract
- 1 cup hot water
- 1/2 cup sour cream

Instructions:

1. Preheat the oven to 350°F (175°C). Grease and flour an 8-inch cake pan.
2. In a large bowl, whisk together flour, baking powder, baking soda, salt, cocoa powder, and sugar.
3. Add eggs, oil, and vanilla extract, mixing until smooth.
4. Gradually add hot water and sour cream, stirring until combined.
5. Pour the batter into the prepared pan.
6. Bake for 25-30 minutes, or until a toothpick comes out clean.
7. Let the cake cool in the pan for 10 minutes, then remove and cool completely before serving.

Chocolate Meringues

Ingredients:

- 4 large egg whites
- 1 cup granulated sugar
- 1 tsp vanilla extract
- 1/4 cup cocoa powder

Instructions:

1. Preheat oven to 225°F (110°C). Line a baking sheet with parchment paper.
2. Beat the egg whites in a bowl until stiff peaks form.
3. Gradually add sugar, beating until glossy and stiff.
4. Gently fold in vanilla and cocoa powder.
5. Spoon or pipe the meringue mixture onto the baking sheet.
6. Bake for 1 hour or until dry and crisp. Let cool before serving.

Chocolate Babka

Ingredients:

- 2 1/2 cups all-purpose flour
- 1/4 cup sugar
- 1 tsp salt
- 1 packet active dry yeast
- 1/2 cup warm milk
- 1/2 cup unsalted butter, softened
- 2 eggs
- 1 cup chocolate chips
- 1/2 cup cocoa powder
- 1/2 cup sugar

Instructions:

1. In a bowl, combine flour, sugar, and salt. In another bowl, dissolve yeast in warm milk and let sit for 5 minutes.
2. Add the yeast mixture, butter, and eggs to the dry ingredients and knead until a dough forms.
3. Let the dough rise for 1 hour.
4. Roll the dough into a rectangle and sprinkle with chocolate chips, cocoa powder, and sugar.
5. Roll the dough tightly and shape it into a loaf.
6. Bake at 350°F (175°C) for 30-35 minutes, until golden brown.

Chocolate Peanut Butter Cups

Ingredients:

- 8 oz semisweet chocolate
- 1/2 cup creamy peanut butter
- 1/4 cup powdered sugar

Instructions:

1. Line a muffin tin with cupcake liners.
2. Melt half of the chocolate and spoon a small amount into each muffin cup, spreading it evenly.
3. Place the tin in the refrigerator for 15 minutes to set the chocolate.
4. Mix peanut butter and powdered sugar together until smooth.
5. Spoon a small amount of peanut butter into each cup on top of the chocolate layer.
6. Melt the remaining chocolate and pour it over the peanut butter layer.
7. Refrigerate for 30 minutes or until the chocolate sets.

Chocolate Ice Cream Sandwiches

Ingredients:

- 1 pint chocolate ice cream
- 24 cookies (chocolate chip, oatmeal, or your favorite variety)
- 1/2 cup mini chocolate chips (optional)

Instructions:

1. Soften the chocolate ice cream slightly by letting it sit at room temperature for a few minutes.
2. Place a scoop of ice cream on the flat side of one cookie.
3. Top with another cookie to form a sandwich.
4. Roll the edges of the ice cream sandwich in mini chocolate chips if desired.
5. Freeze for at least 1 hour before serving.

Chocolate Coconut Macaroons

Ingredients:

- 2 1/2 cups shredded coconut
- 1/2 cup sweetened condensed milk
- 1/4 cup cocoa powder
- 1 tsp vanilla extract
- 1/4 tsp salt
- 8 oz semisweet chocolate, chopped

Instructions:

1. Preheat oven to 350°F (175°C). Line a baking sheet with parchment paper.
2. In a bowl, mix coconut, condensed milk, cocoa powder, vanilla, and salt.
3. Form the mixture into small mounds and place them on the baking sheet.
4. Bake for 12-15 minutes until golden brown.
5. Let cool completely, then dip in melted chocolate and refrigerate until the chocolate sets.

Chocolate Covered Almonds

Ingredients:

- 1 cup raw almonds
- 8 oz semisweet chocolate
- 1 tsp vanilla extract (optional)

Instructions:

1. Toast the almonds in a preheated oven at 350°F (175°C) for 10-12 minutes, or until fragrant. Let cool.
2. Melt the chocolate in a microwave-safe bowl or over a double boiler.
3. Stir in vanilla extract, if using.
4. Dip each almond into the melted chocolate and place on parchment paper.
5. Let the chocolate set at room temperature or refrigerate until firm.

Chocolate Biscotti

Ingredients:

- 1 3/4 cups all-purpose flour
- 1 cup sugar
- 1/2 cup unsweetened cocoa powder
- 1 tsp baking powder
- 1/2 tsp salt
- 2 large eggs
- 1 tsp vanilla extract
- 1/2 cup semisweet chocolate chips
- 1/2 cup almonds, chopped (optional)

Instructions:

1. Preheat oven to 350°F (175°C). Line a baking sheet with parchment paper.
2. In a large bowl, whisk together flour, sugar, cocoa powder, baking powder, and salt.
3. In a separate bowl, whisk eggs and vanilla. Add to dry ingredients and mix until a dough forms.
4. Stir in chocolate chips and almonds.
5. Shape dough into a log on the baking sheet and flatten slightly.
6. Bake for 25 minutes. Remove from the oven and let cool slightly.
7. Slice into 1/2-inch pieces and bake for an additional 10-15 minutes until crisp.

Chocolate Dipped Marshmallows

Ingredients:

- 10 marshmallows
- 4 oz semisweet chocolate
- Sprinkles, crushed nuts, or coconut (optional)

Instructions:

1. Melt the chocolate in a microwave-safe bowl or over a double boiler.
2. Insert a toothpick into each marshmallow.
3. Dip each marshmallow into the melted chocolate, coating it halfway or entirely.
4. Roll in sprinkles or crushed nuts, if desired.
5. Place on parchment paper and refrigerate until the chocolate sets, about 30 minutes.

Chocolate Chip Scones

Ingredients:

- 2 cups all-purpose flour
- 1/4 cup sugar
- 2 1/2 tsp baking powder
- 1/2 tsp salt
- 1/2 cup unsalted butter, cold and cubed
- 1/2 cup chocolate chips
- 1/2 cup heavy cream
- 1 egg
- 1 tsp vanilla extract

Instructions:

1. Preheat oven to 400°F (200°C). Line a baking sheet with parchment paper.
2. In a bowl, combine flour, sugar, baking powder, and salt.
3. Add butter and cut it into the dry ingredients using a pastry cutter until it resembles coarse crumbs.
4. Stir in chocolate chips.
5. In a separate bowl, whisk together cream, egg, and vanilla.
6. Add wet ingredients to the dry ingredients and mix until just combined.
7. Turn the dough onto a floured surface and gently knead. Shape into a disk and cut into 8 wedges.
8. Place on a baking sheet and bake for 15-18 minutes, until golden brown.

Chocolate Hazelnut Spread

Ingredients:

- 1 cup hazelnuts, toasted
- 1/2 cup powdered sugar
- 1/4 cup cocoa powder
- 1/4 tsp salt
- 2 tbsp vegetable oil
- 1 tsp vanilla extract
- 1/2 cup semisweet chocolate, melted

Instructions:

1. Blend toasted hazelnuts in a food processor until smooth.
2. Add powdered sugar, cocoa powder, salt, oil, and vanilla, and blend until combined.
3. Stir in the melted chocolate until smooth.
4. Store in an airtight container at room temperature.

7. Cool completely before frosting.

Chocolate Mocha Cake

Ingredients:

- 1 3/4 cups all-purpose flour
- 1/2 cup cocoa powder
- 1 tsp baking powder
- 1/2 tsp baking soda
- 1/4 tsp salt
- 1/2 cup brewed coffee
- 1/2 cup buttermilk
- 1 cup sugar
- 1/2 cup unsalted butter, softened
- 2 large eggs
- 1 tsp vanilla extract
- 1/2 cup semisweet chocolate chips

Instructions:

1. Preheat oven to 350°F (175°C). Grease and flour an 8-inch cake pan.
2. Mix flour, cocoa powder, baking powder, baking soda, and salt.
3. In another bowl, beat sugar and butter until fluffy, then add eggs, coffee, buttermilk, and vanilla.
4. Gradually add dry ingredients to wet, mixing until smooth.
5. Fold in chocolate chips.
6. Pour into the cake pan and bake for 30-35 minutes.

Chocolate Panna Cotta

Ingredients:

- 1 1/2 cups heavy cream
- 1/2 cup whole milk
- 1/2 cup sugar
- 1 tsp vanilla extract
- 8 oz semisweet chocolate, chopped
- 1 packet gelatin

Instructions:

1. Sprinkle gelatin over cold milk and let sit for 5 minutes.
2. Heat cream and sugar in a saucepan until the sugar dissolves and it starts to simmer.
3. Stir in the gelatin mixture until dissolved.
4. Add chopped chocolate and stir until melted and smooth.
5. Pour into individual cups and chill for at least 4 hours until set.

Chocolate Popcorn

Ingredients:

- 1/2 cup popcorn kernels
- 8 oz semisweet chocolate
- 1/4 cup white chocolate (optional)
- Sea salt (optional)

Instructions:

1. Pop the popcorn using your preferred method and spread it onto a parchment-lined baking sheet.
2. Melt the semisweet chocolate in a microwave or over a double boiler.
3. Drizzle the melted chocolate over the popcorn.
4. Melt the white chocolate and drizzle it over the dark chocolate if desired.
5. Sprinkle with a little sea salt if using.
6. Let the chocolate set for 1 hour before serving.

Chocolate Coconut Balls

Ingredients:

- 2 cups shredded coconut
- 1/2 cup powdered sugar
- 1/4 cup sweetened condensed milk
- 1/2 tsp vanilla extract
- 8 oz semisweet chocolate, chopped

Instructions:

1. In a bowl, mix coconut, powdered sugar, condensed milk, and vanilla until combined.
2. Roll into small balls and place on a parchment-lined tray.
3. Chill in the fridge for 30 minutes.
4. Melt the chocolate and dip each coconut ball into the chocolate.
5. Refrigerate again for 30 minutes until the chocolate is set.

Chocolate Covered Pretzels

Ingredients:

- 12 oz semisweet chocolate
- 1 bag mini pretzels
- 1 tbsp vegetable oil (optional for smoother chocolate)

Instructions:

1. Melt the chocolate and oil (if using) in a microwave-safe bowl or over a double boiler.
2. Dip pretzels into the melted chocolate, then place them on a parchment-lined baking sheet.
3. Refrigerate for 30 minutes until the chocolate sets.
4. Serve as a sweet and salty snack.

Chocolate Chip Pancakes

Ingredients:

- 1 1/2 cups all-purpose flour
- 2 tbsp sugar
- 1 tsp baking powder
- 1/2 tsp baking soda
- 1/4 tsp salt
- 1 cup buttermilk
- 1 large egg
- 2 tbsp unsalted butter, melted
- 1/2 cup chocolate chips
- Butter or oil for cooking

Instructions:

1. In a bowl, whisk together flour, sugar, baking powder, baking soda, and salt.
2. In a separate bowl, whisk together buttermilk, egg, and melted butter.
3. Pour the wet ingredients into the dry ingredients and stir until just combined.
4. Fold in chocolate chips.
5. Heat a skillet over medium heat and cook pancakes, flipping once bubbles form.
6. Serve with syrup or more chocolate chips.

Chocolate Ganache

Ingredients:

- 8 oz semisweet chocolate, chopped
- 1 cup heavy cream
- 1 tbsp unsalted butter (optional)

Instructions:

1. Heat the cream in a saucepan over medium heat until it begins to simmer.
2. Pour the hot cream over the chopped chocolate. Let it sit for 3-5 minutes.
3. Stir until smooth. If desired, add butter for extra richness.
4. Let the ganache cool slightly before using as a glaze or frosting.

7. Bake for 50-60 minutes until set. Let cool, then refrigerate for at least 4 hours before serving.

Chocolate and Raspberry Tart

Ingredients:

- 1 1/2 cups graham cracker crumbs
- 1/4 cup sugar
- 1/2 cup butter, melted
- 8 oz dark chocolate
- 1/2 cup heavy cream
- 1 tsp vanilla extract
- 1 cup fresh raspberries

Instructions:

1. Preheat the oven to 350°F (175°C). Press the graham cracker crumbs, sugar, and melted butter into the bottom of a tart pan.
2. Bake for 10 minutes, then let cool.
3. In a saucepan, heat heavy cream until simmering. Remove from heat and add dark chocolate, stirring until melted and smooth.
4. Stir in vanilla extract.
5. Pour the chocolate mixture into the cooled crust and refrigerate for at least 2 hours.
6. Top with fresh raspberries before serving.

Chocolate Coconut Pudding

Ingredients:

- 2 cups coconut milk
- 1/2 cup sugar
- 3 tbsp cornstarch
- 1/4 tsp salt
- 3 oz dark chocolate, chopped
- 1 tsp vanilla extract

Instructions:

1. In a saucepan, combine coconut milk, sugar, cornstarch, and salt. Bring to a simmer, whisking constantly.
2. Once thickened, remove from heat and stir in chopped dark chocolate and vanilla.
3. Pour into serving bowls and refrigerate for 2 hours until set.
4. Top with shredded coconut before serving.

Chocolate Almond Bark

Ingredients:

- 8 oz dark chocolate
- 1/2 cup sliced almonds
- 1/4 cup dried cranberries (optional)

Instructions:

1. Melt the dark chocolate in a microwave-safe bowl or over a double boiler.
2. Stir in sliced almonds and dried cranberries if using.
3. Pour the mixture onto a baking sheet lined with parchment paper and spread it out evenly.
4. Refrigerate for 30 minutes until set, then break into pieces.

Chocolate Coconut Truffles

Ingredients:

- 8 oz dark chocolate
- 1/2 cup heavy cream
- 1/2 cup shredded coconut
- 1 tsp vanilla extract

Instructions:

1. In a saucepan, heat the heavy cream until simmering. Pour over chopped dark chocolate and stir until smooth.
2. Stir in vanilla extract and shredded coconut.
3. Refrigerate for 2 hours until firm.
4. Roll into balls and coat with additional shredded coconut.
5. Refrigerate again for 30 minutes before serving.

Chocolate Chip Banana Bread

Ingredients:

- 2 ripe bananas, mashed
- 1/2 cup melted butter
- 1 cup sugar
- 1 egg
- 1 tsp vanilla extract
- 1 1/2 cups all-purpose flour
- 1 tsp baking soda
- 1/4 tsp salt
- 1/2 cup chocolate chips

Instructions:

1. Preheat oven to 350°F (175°C). Grease a loaf pan.
2. In a bowl, mix mashed bananas, melted butter, sugar, egg, and vanilla.
3. In a separate bowl, whisk together flour, baking soda, and salt.
4. Gradually add the dry ingredients to the banana mixture and stir until combined.
5. Fold in chocolate chips.
6. Pour the batter into the loaf pan and bake for 60-65 minutes until a toothpick comes out clean.
7. Let cool before slicing.

Chocolate Cheesecake Bars

Ingredients:

- 1 1/2 cups graham cracker crumbs
- 1/4 cup sugar
- 1/2 cup butter, melted
- 2 packages (8 oz) cream cheese, softened
- 1/2 cup sugar
- 1 tsp vanilla extract
- 2 eggs
- 8 oz dark chocolate, melted

Instructions:

1. Preheat oven to 325°F (160°C). Grease a 9x13-inch baking dish.
2. Mix graham cracker crumbs, sugar, and melted butter. Press into the bottom of the dish.
3. In a bowl, beat cream cheese, sugar, and vanilla until smooth. Add eggs one at a time, mixing well.
4. Stir in melted chocolate.
5. Pour the mixture over the crust and bake for 35-40 minutes until set.
6. Let cool and refrigerate for 2 hours before cutting into bars.

Chocolate Chia Pudding

Ingredients:

- 2 cups almond milk
- 1/4 cup chia seeds
- 3 tbsp cocoa powder
- 2 tbsp maple syrup
- 1 tsp vanilla extract

Instructions:

1. In a bowl, whisk together almond milk, chia seeds, cocoa powder, maple syrup, and vanilla extract.
2. Refrigerate for at least 4 hours or overnight to allow the chia seeds to absorb the liquid and thicken.
3. Stir before serving and top with fresh berries if desired.

Chocolate Tiramisu

Ingredients:

- 1 package ladyfingers
- 1 1/2 cups heavy cream
- 1/2 cup mascarpone cheese
- 1/2 cup sugar
- 1 tsp vanilla extract
- 1/4 cup espresso or strong coffee
- 2 tbsp cocoa powder
- 4 oz dark chocolate, grated

Instructions:

1. In a bowl, whip heavy cream, mascarpone cheese, sugar, and vanilla extract until stiff peaks form.
2. Dip ladyfingers into espresso and layer them in the bottom of a dish.
3. Spread a layer of the mascarpone mixture over the ladyfingers.
4. Repeat the layers, then refrigerate for 2 hours.
5. Dust with cocoa powder and grated chocolate before serving.

Chocolate Pretzel Bark

Ingredients:

- 8 oz semisweet chocolate
- 1 cup pretzels, broken into pieces
- 1/2 cup mini chocolate chips (optional)
- 1/4 cup caramel sauce (optional)

Instructions:

1. Line a baking sheet with parchment paper.
2. Melt the semisweet chocolate in a microwave-safe bowl or over a double boiler.
3. Spread the melted chocolate onto the prepared baking sheet, smoothing it out into an even layer.
4. Sprinkle the broken pretzels over the chocolate, gently pressing them down.
5. Optionally, drizzle with caramel sauce and sprinkle mini chocolate chips on top.
6. Refrigerate for at least 1 hour, or until the chocolate has set.
7. Break into pieces and serve.

Chocolate Almond Croissants

Ingredients:

- 1 sheet puff pastry (store-bought or homemade)
- 1/2 cup chocolate chips
- 1/4 cup slivered almonds
- 1 egg (for egg wash)
- 2 tbsp sugar (for sprinkling)

Instructions:

1. Preheat oven to 400°F (200°C). Line a baking sheet with parchment paper.
2. Roll out the puff pastry sheet on a lightly floured surface.
3. Cut the pastry into 4-6 equal-sized rectangles.
4. Place chocolate chips and slivered almonds in the center of each rectangle.
5. Fold the edges of the pastry over the filling to form a triangle or rectangular shape, sealing the edges.
6. Beat the egg and brush the tops of the croissants with the egg wash.
7. Sprinkle with sugar.
8. Bake for 15-20 minutes, until golden brown and puffed.
9. Let cool slightly before serving.

Chocolate Soufflé Cake

Ingredients:

- 4 oz semisweet chocolate
- 1/2 cup unsalted butter
- 1/2 cup sugar
- 3 large eggs, separated
- 1/4 cup all-purpose flour
- 1/2 tsp vanilla extract
- 1/4 tsp salt
- Powdered sugar, for dusting

Instructions:

1. Preheat oven to 375°F (190°C). Grease a 9-inch round cake pan and dust it with flour.
2. Melt the chocolate and butter together in a heatproof bowl over simmering water or in the microwave.
3. In a separate bowl, whisk the egg yolks and sugar together until light and fluffy.
4. Stir in the melted chocolate mixture, followed by the flour, vanilla, and salt.
5. In another bowl, beat the egg whites until stiff peaks form.
6. Gently fold the egg whites into the chocolate mixture until fully combined.
7. Pour the batter into the prepared cake pan and bake for 25-30 minutes, or until the top is set but slightly soft in the center.
8. Dust with powdered sugar and serve warm.

www.ingramcontent.com/pod-product-compliance
Lightning Source LLC
LaVergne TN
LVHW061950070526
838199LV00060B/4053